Gorgeous Coloring Book NARWHAL

THIS BOOK

BELONGS TO

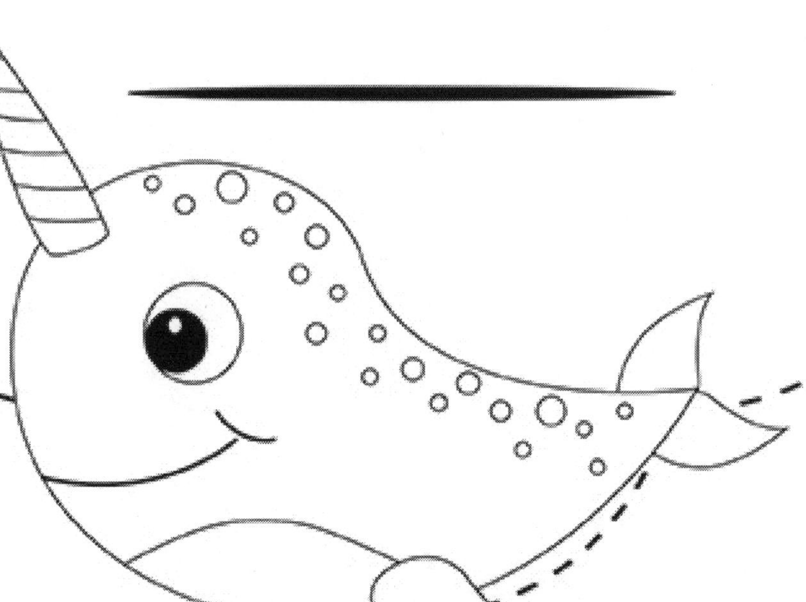

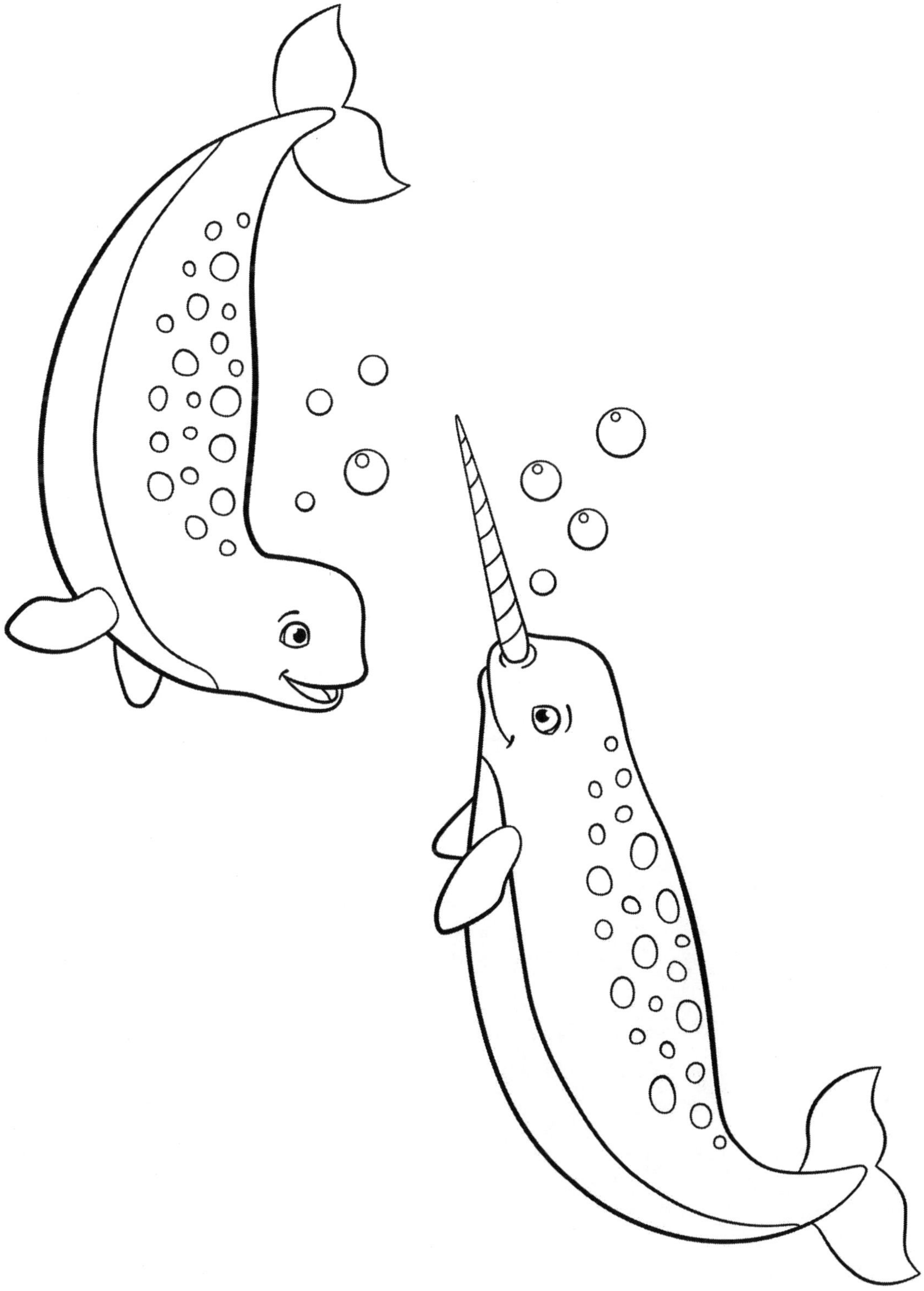

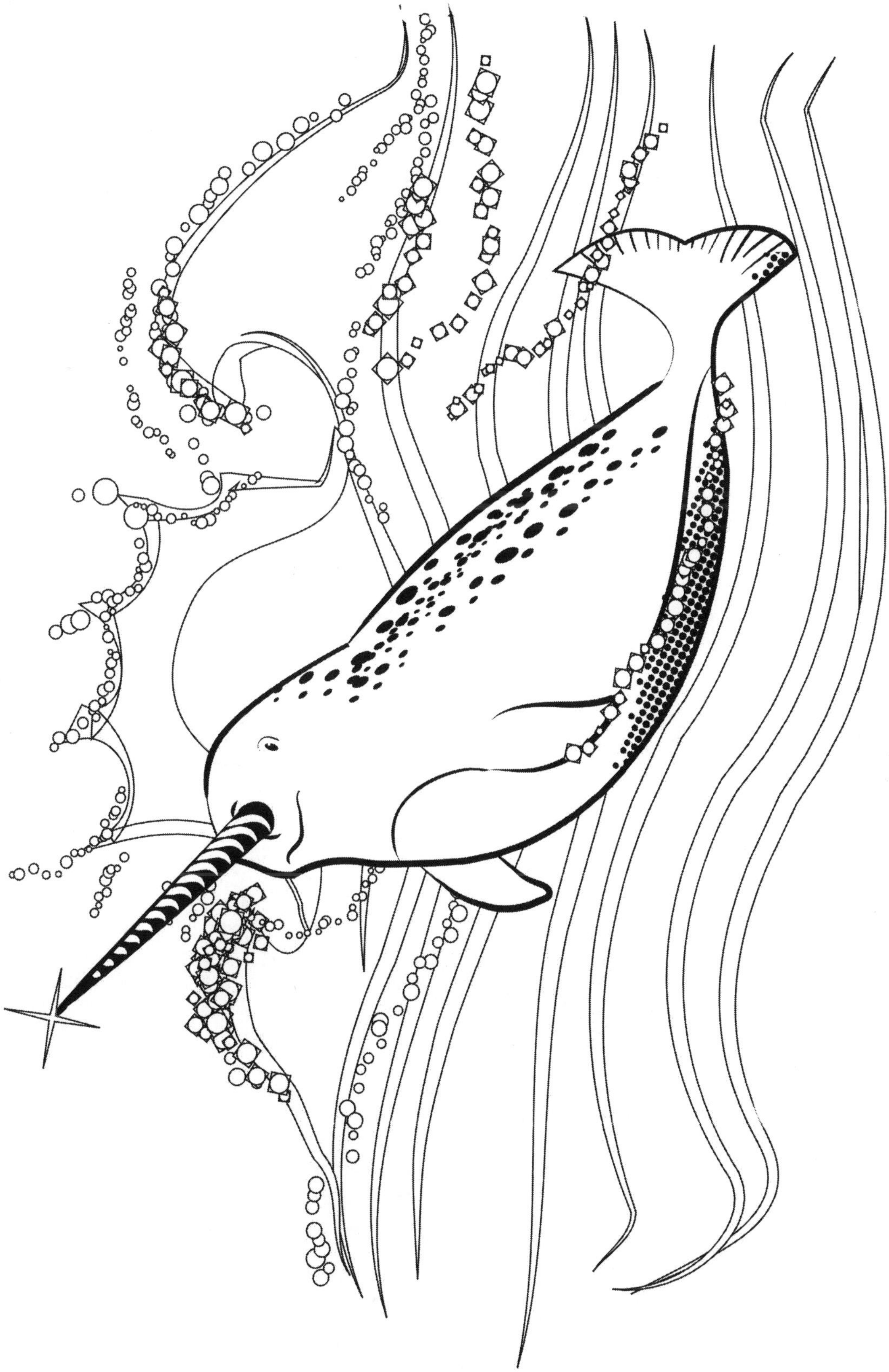

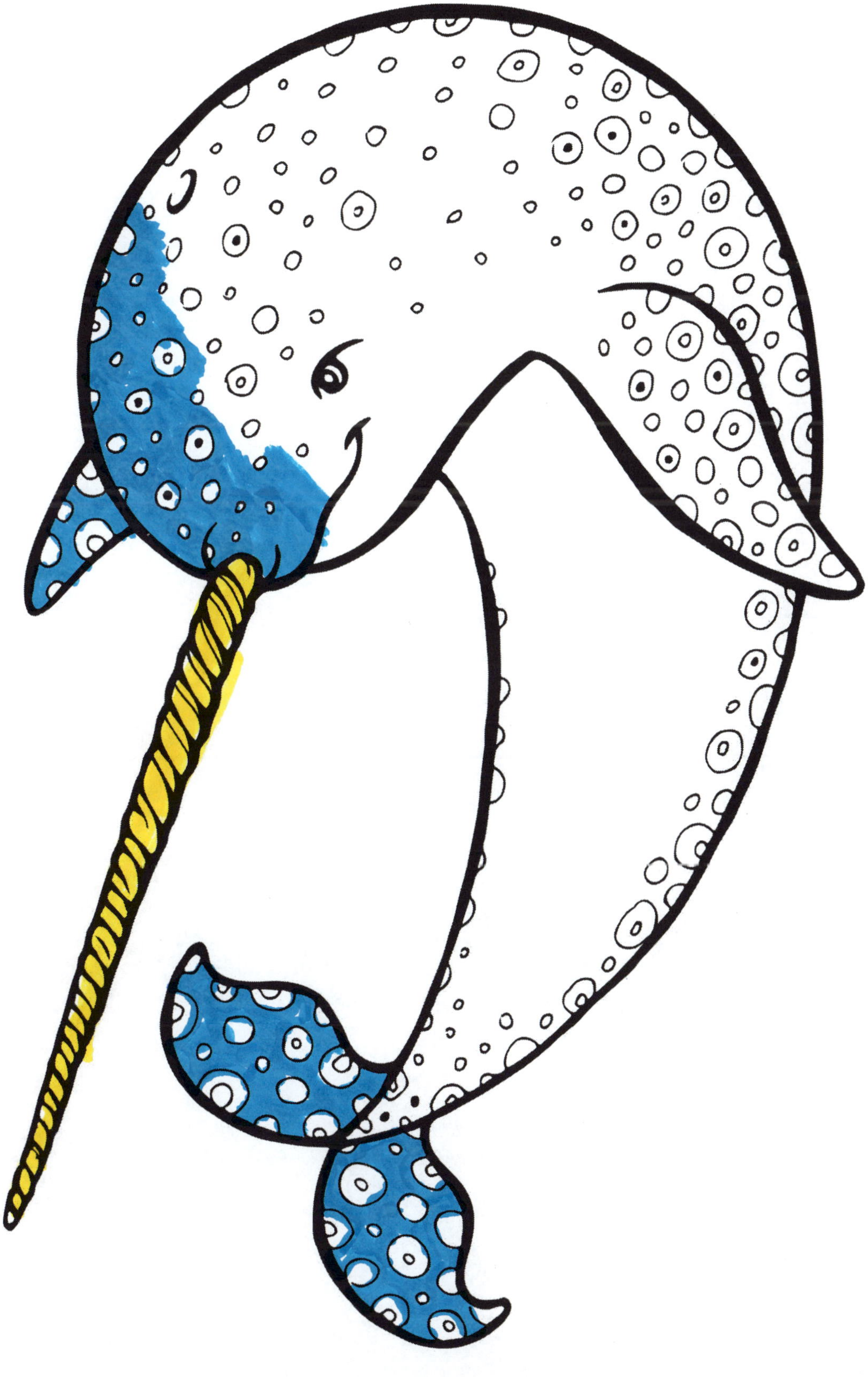

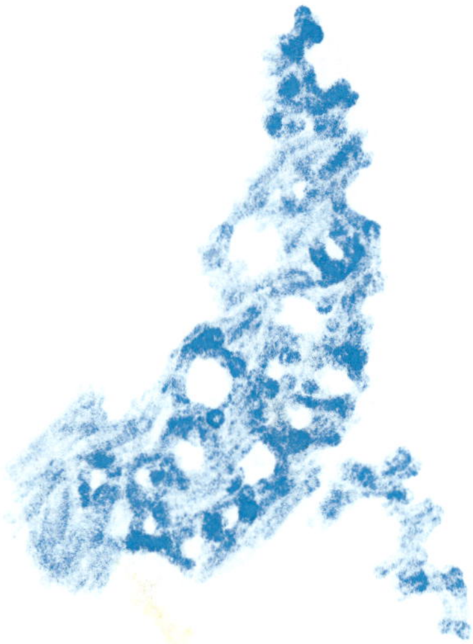

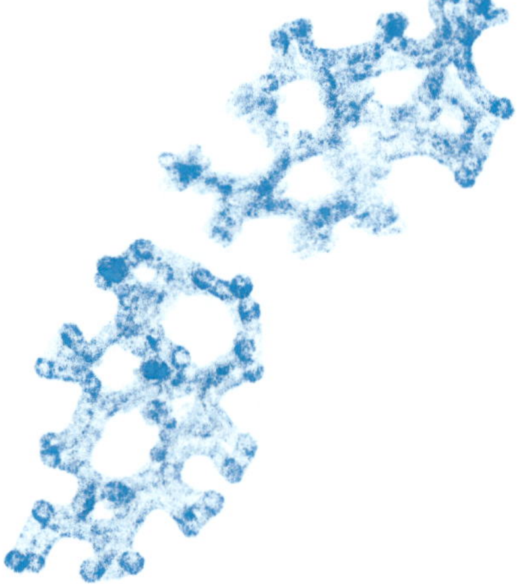

This Book
Belongs to:
____

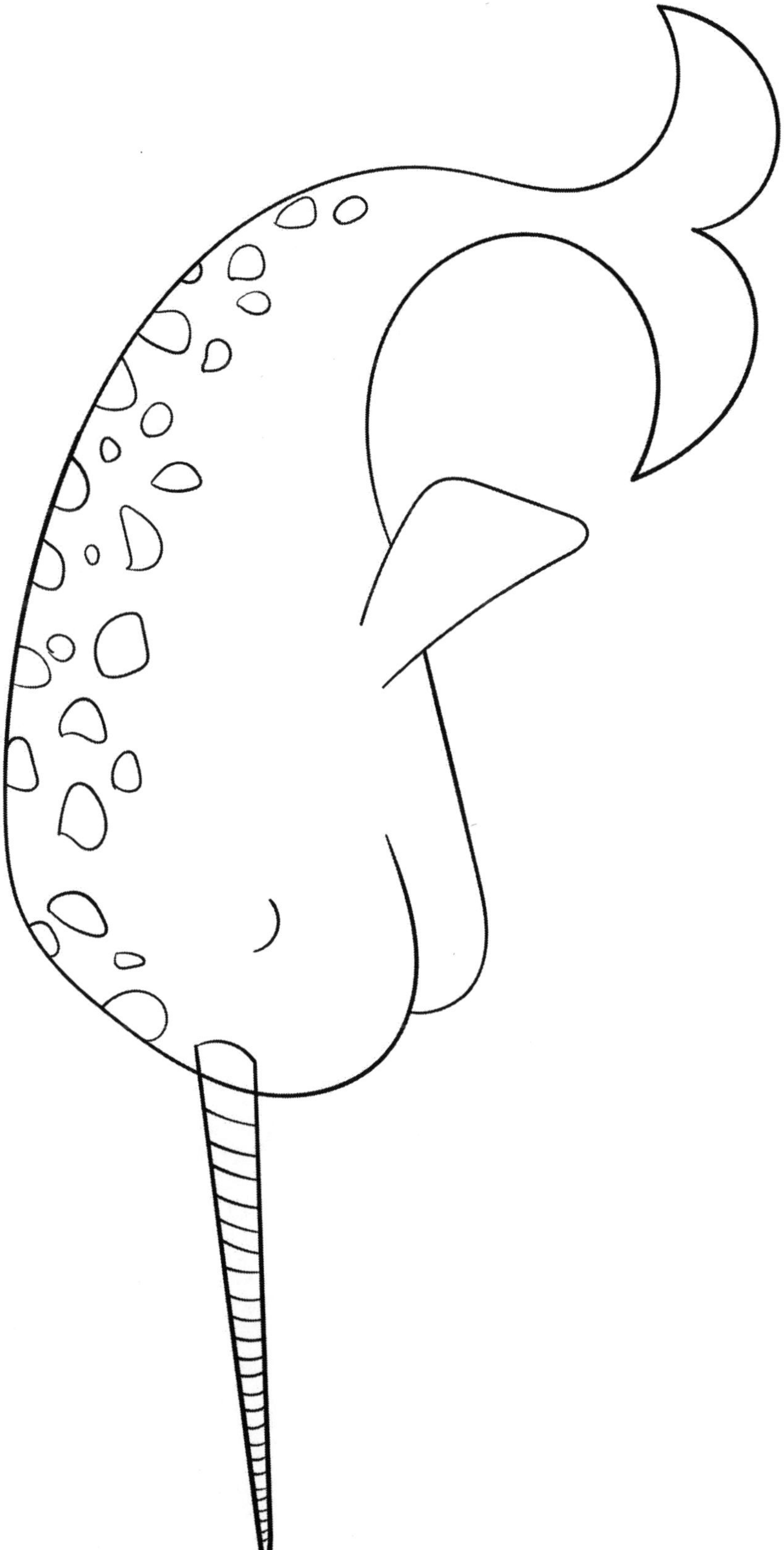

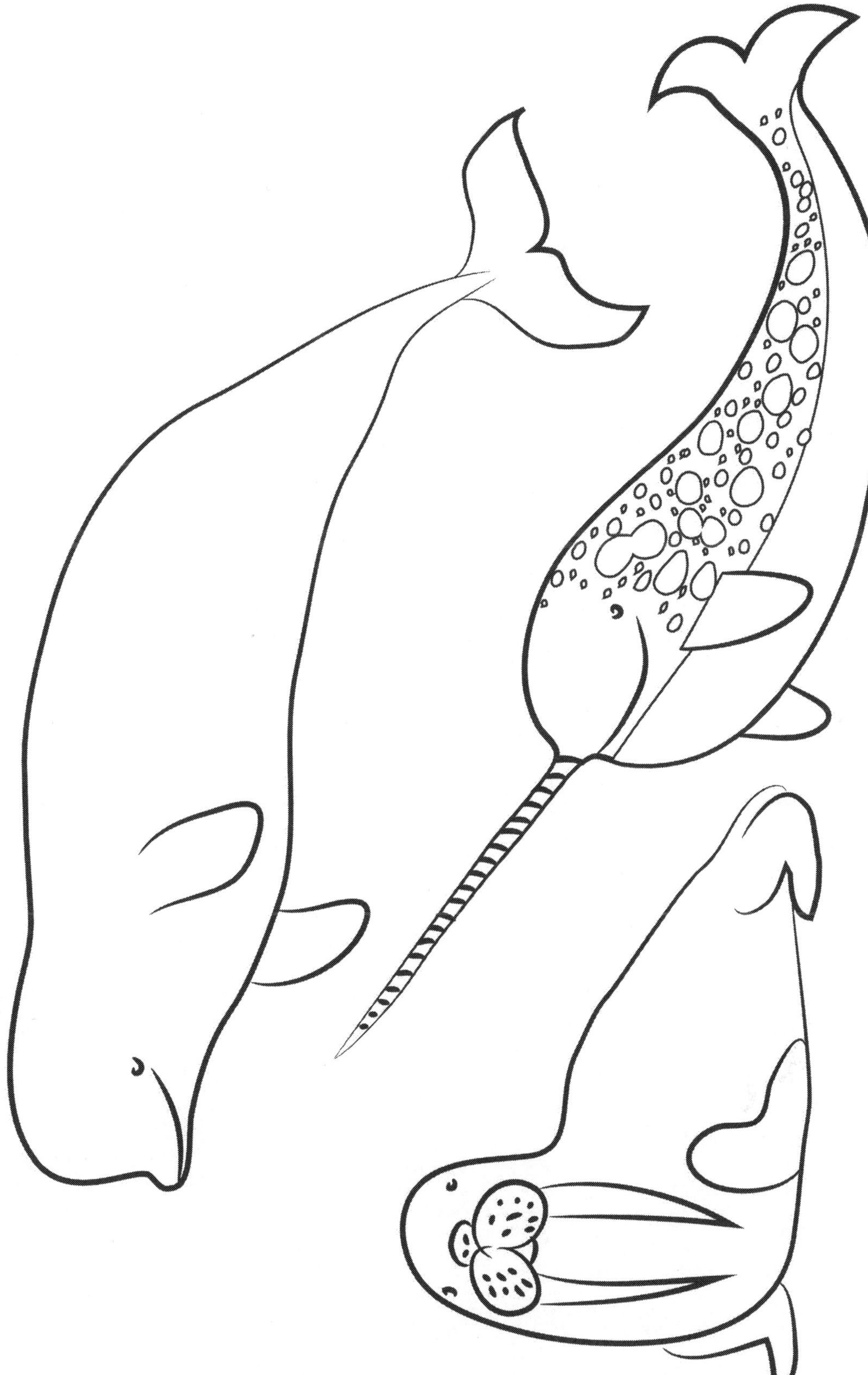

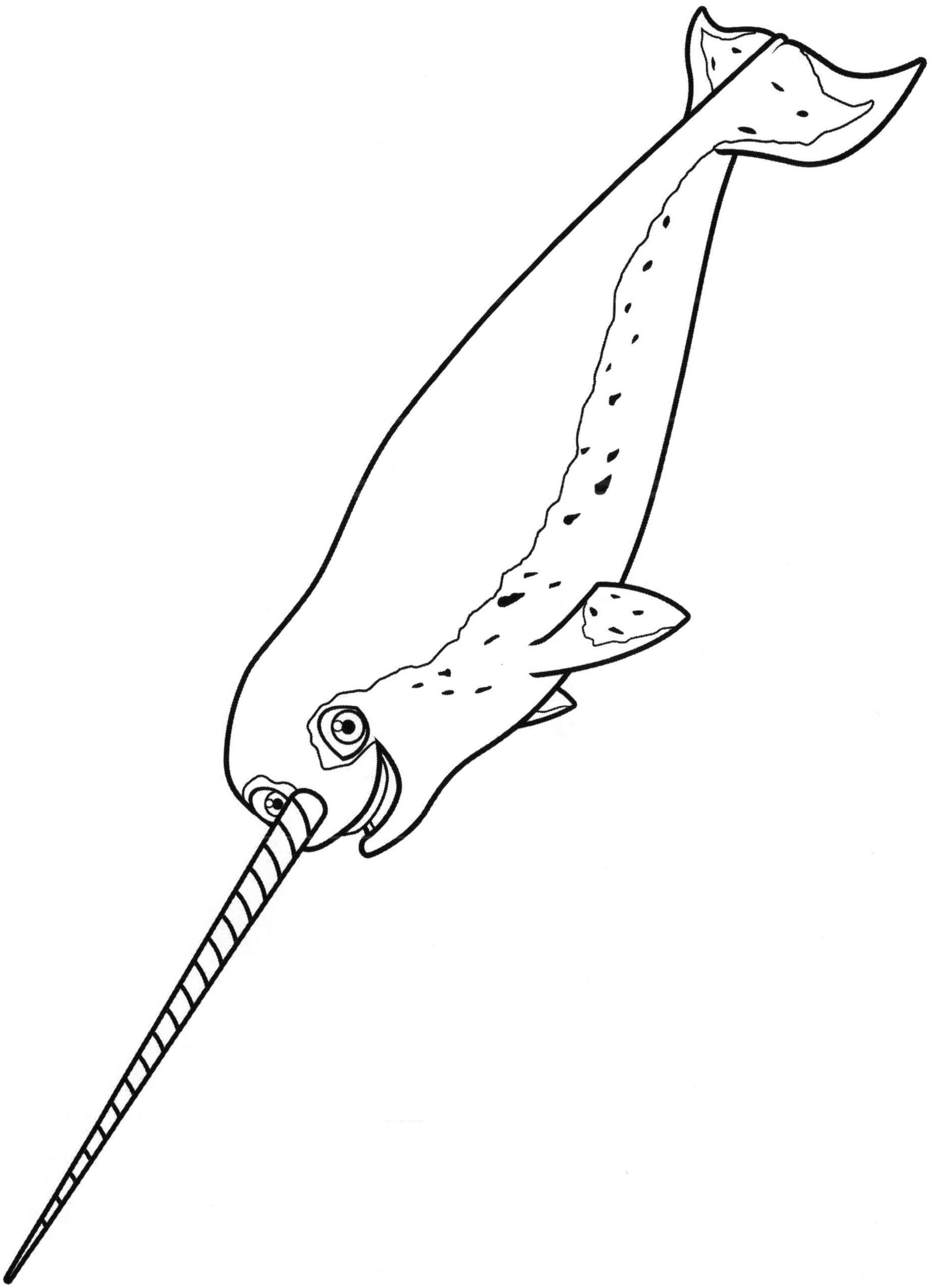

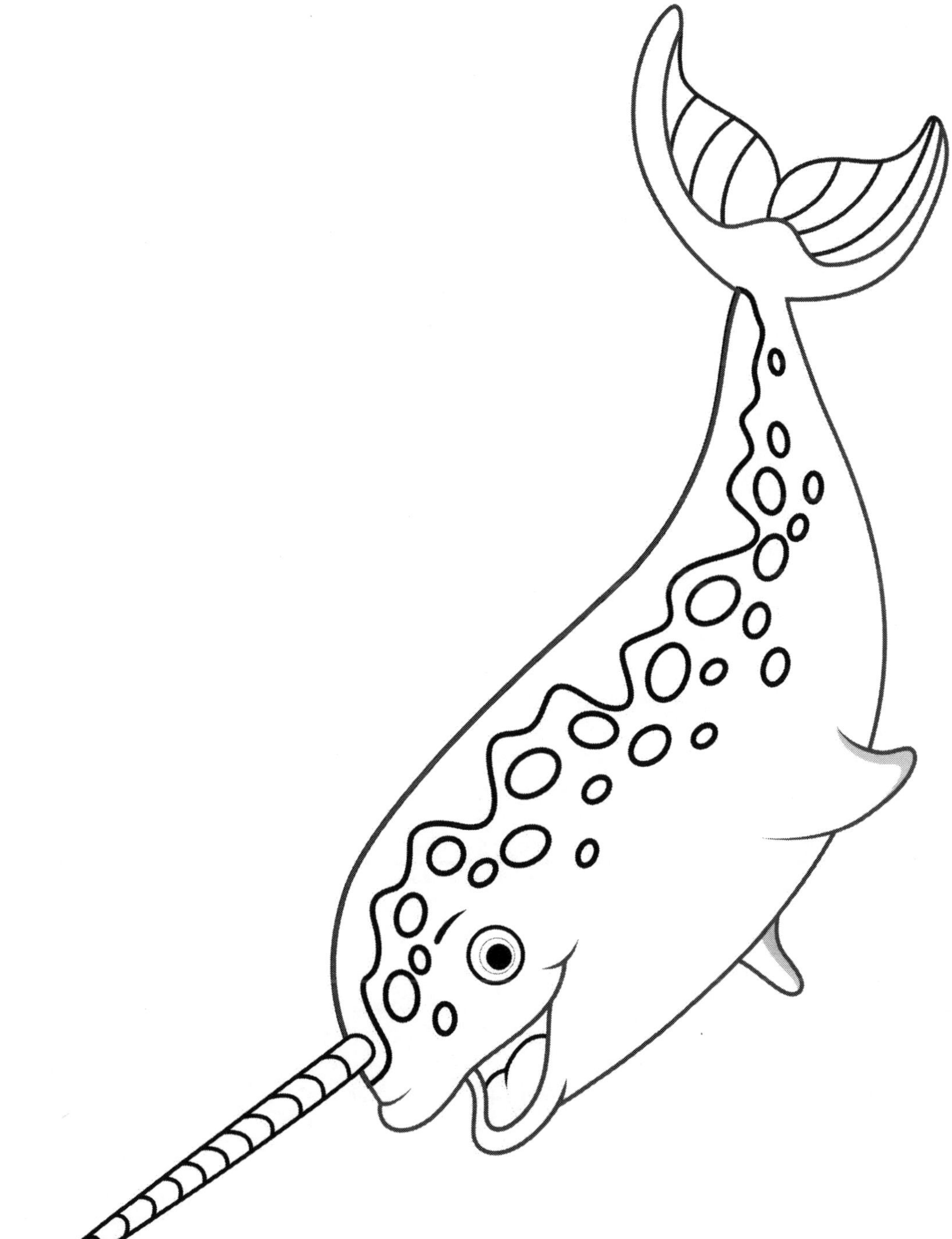

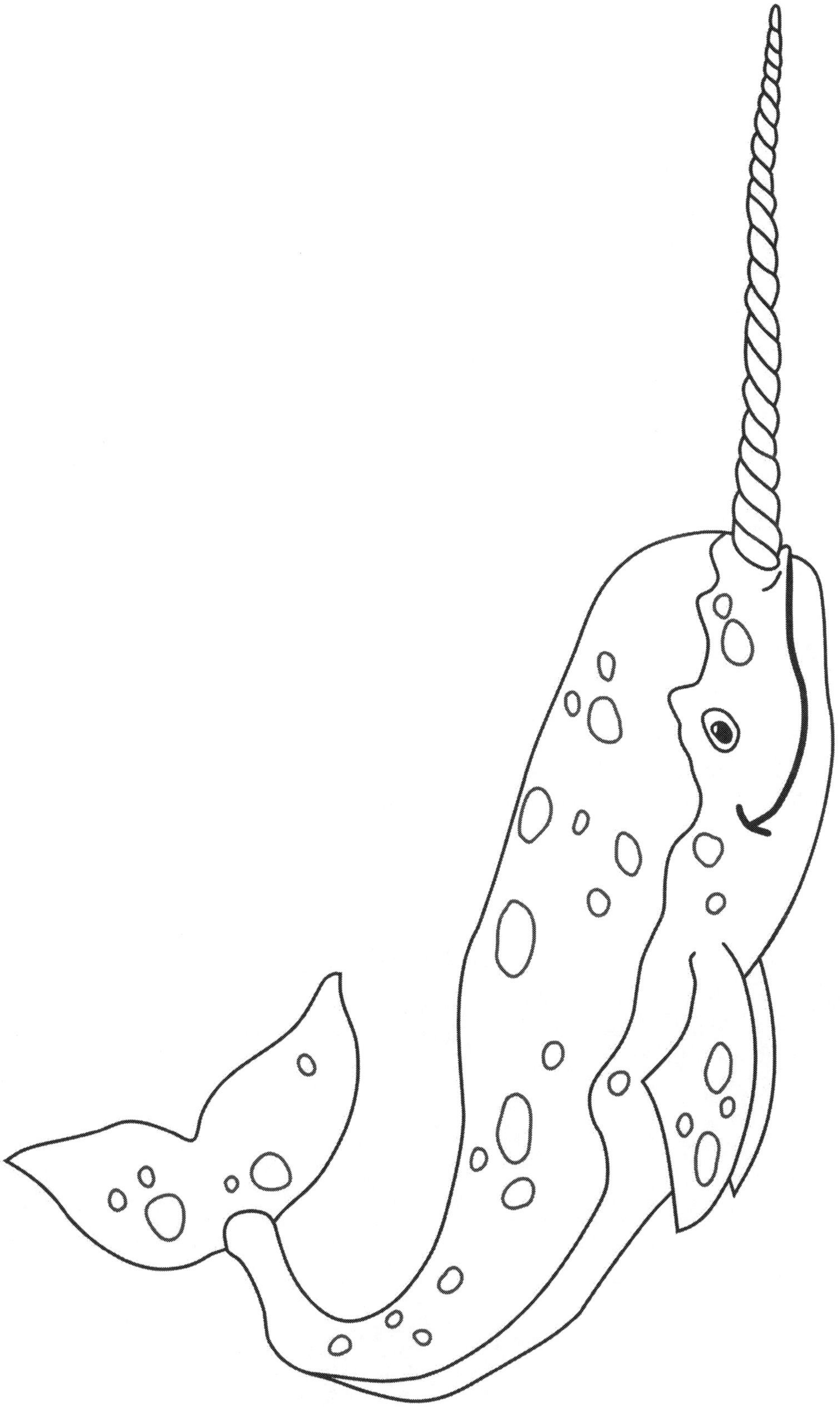

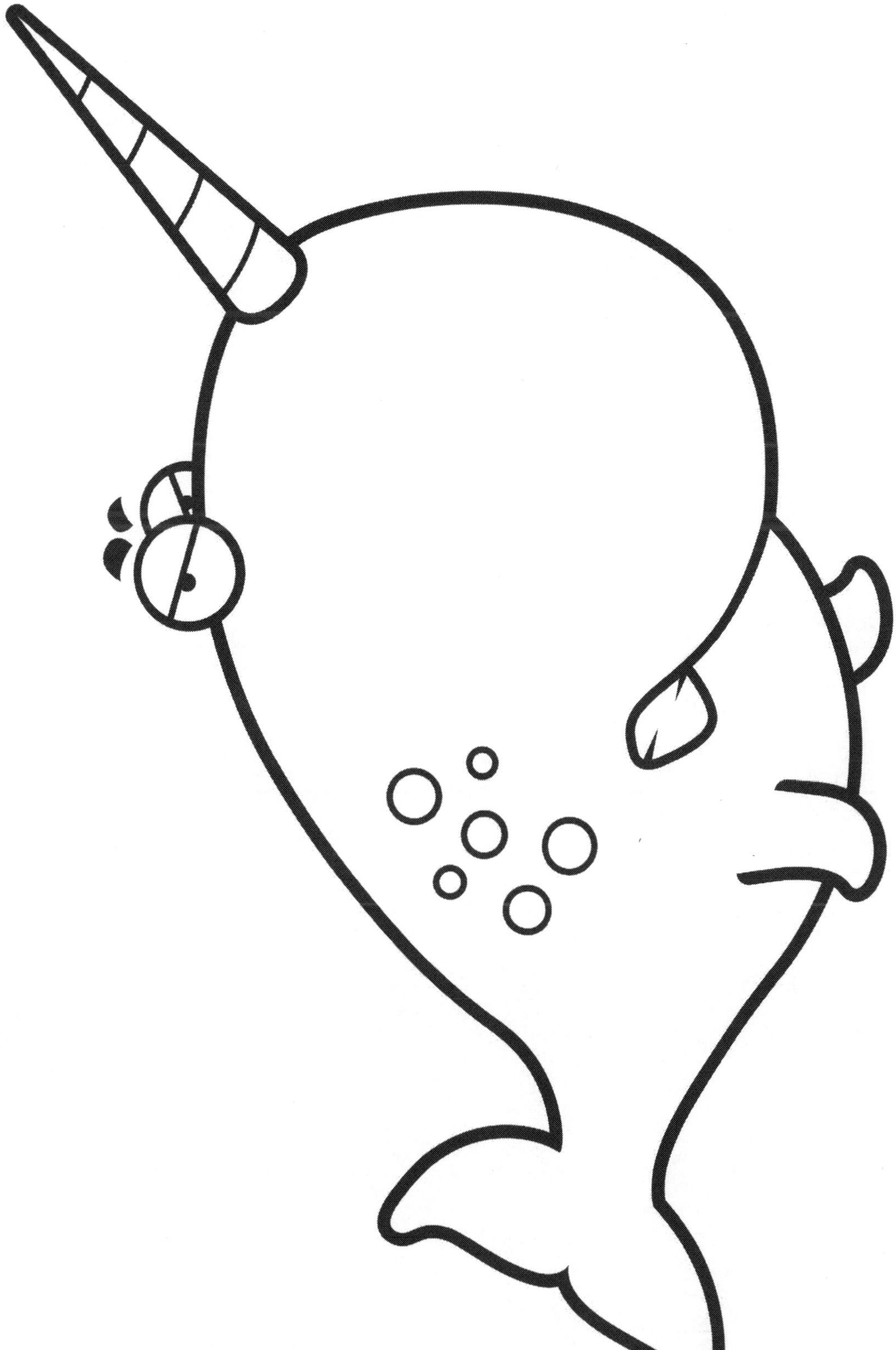

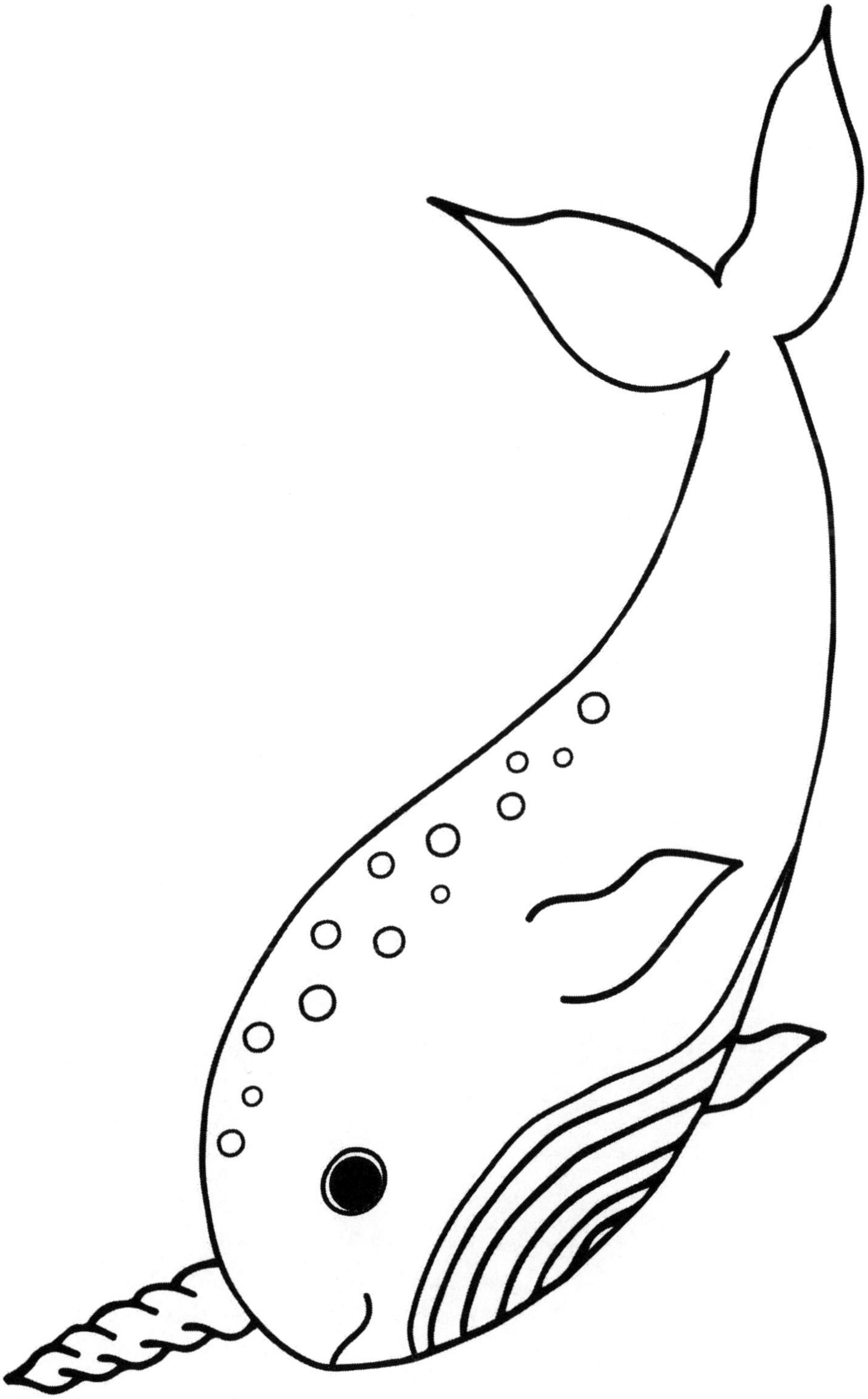

16932887R00035

Made in the USA
Lexington, KY
17 November 2018